MAGNIFICENT MACHINES

Chosen by John Foster

Illustrated by Peter Allen

MACMILLAN CHILDREN'S BOOKS

First published 2000
by Macmillan Children's Books

This edition published 2001
by Macmillan Children's Books
a division of Pan Macmillan Limited
20 New Wharf Road, London N1 9RR
Basingstoke and Oxford
www.panmacmillan.com

Associated companies throughout the world

ISBN 0 330 39145 3

135798642

A CIP catalogue record for this book is available from the British Library

Printed and bound by Mackays of Chatham plc, Kent

Contents

Machines, Machines

Machines,
   machines, machines everywhere.
One hoovers the house.
   One dries your wet hair.

Machines,
   machines all over the place.
Some roar down the road.
   Some orbit in space.

Machines,
   machines, machines big and small.
One hums while you sleep.
   One ticks in the hall.

Wes Magee

Grandad's Gadget

Grandad built a gadget made of
tweezers, hooks and springs.
"My little gadget," Grandad said,
"can mend just anything.
So bring your broken toys along,
broken china too.
Then press this button. My machine
will make them good as new!"
We brought a pile of toys along.
My best friend brought a bike.
"That's right," said Grandad, "form a queue.
Bring anything you like."
But the gadget built more gadgets from
the broken, battered toys
which ran about on little legs
around the girls and boys.
Then they rushed at Grandad
on their tiny, twinkling feet
and Grandad hopped and shouted as
they chased him down the street.

Marian Swinger

2

Snack Attack

I went up to the crisp machine
And put in 20p,
It shook its metal frame and winked
Its price display at me.

It said, "I know you've asked me for
A bacon crunchy snack,
But if you're interested I've got
Some specials round the back.

I've got some choc chip grasshoppers
And ready salted fleas,
And jelly-coated millipedes
And toffee bumble bees.

Or if you fancy something
That's a little bit more filling
I've got some ice cream hedgehogs
In the freezer section, chilling."

I thanked him for his offer
But I suddenly felt sickly,
I said, "I've just remembered
That I need to get home quickly,

And though I do not doubt
That jelly millipedes are yummy,
I think I'll stick to boring choc chip
Cookies baked by Mummy."

Julia Rawlinson

Waving at Trains

I like to wave at trains
as they hurry down the track,
but when I stick my tongue out
nobody waves back.

Brian Moses

Dust Cart

The dust cart is a smelly beast
Its breath is stale and bitter
But then again, yours would be too
If all you ate was litter.

Richard Caley

Abdul's Carpet

They couldn't believe it
when little Abdul
flew past on a carpet
and landed at school.

"My Gran made the carpet,"
said little Abdul,
"so I could fly quickly
and safely to school."

The teacher asked Granny
to come to the school
and make a few carpets
with little Abdul.

Now all of the children
fly carpets to school,
thanks to the Granny
of little Abdul.

Marian Swinger

The Dream Machine

It is woven from
the sparkling threads
of a thousand rainbows
so that when it
sways and swirls
in the midnight air
curtains of feathered light
dance over
the rooftops of the world
and sprinkle
painted dreams
into the sleeping heads
of children.

Cynthia Rider

Vac

Our vacuum cleaner
Sucked up the cat
The morning paper
The kitchen mat
Two dozen spiders
A pair of shoes
A vest and panties
(I'm not sure whose)
Some CDs and
Cassettes galore
A nest of tables
The bathroom door
The electric cooker
The TV set
An ancient poster
Of 'Wet, Wet, Wet'
Our neighbour's dog
The postman, too
Our dining chairs
The upstairs loo
Some plastic bricks
And – what a drag!
I think it needs
A change of bag . . .

Trevor Harvey

The Haunted House

There's a monster haunts our house –
It's called the central heating.
From the way its stomach rumbles,
Goodness knows what it's been eating.

It wakes us up at night-time
With its gurglings and its groanings,
Its clattering and its clanging,
Its mutterings and moanings.

Mum says it lives on water,
In answer to my question.
I think that it must gulp it down
To get such indigestion!

John Foster

glug glug
glug
gurgle

Lawnmower

I want to be a lawnmower –
I like the smell of grass.
I want to feel the buttercups
And daisies brushing past.

I know I get all sneezy
In the sun, but I suppose
That if I was a lawnmower
I wouldn't have a nose.

Julia Rawlinson

Dodgems

Bumpers bashing
Bright sparks flashing
Darting, dashing everywhere
Thrilling, smashing
Buggies crashing
Ride the dodgems at the fair.

Richard Caley

Space Rocket

Super, shiny space rocket
Shoot me to the stars
Land me safely on the Moon
Then carry me to Mars.

Fire me into orbit
Beyond the Milky Way
Then loop the loop through Saturn's rings
What fun we'll have today.

Take me to the planets
That no one else has seen
Like Jupiter with golden clouds
Or Pluto shining green.

Super, shiny space rocket
Please let me fly with you
Together we can cruise the sky
And make my dreams come true.

Richard Caley

The HUMAN Machine

The very most brilliant
Machine that there's been
Is quite without question
The HUMAN machine.

For thousands of years
This machine's been around,
But it beats all the modern ones
Into the ground.

For this machine runs
And it jumps and it walks,
It sings and it thinks
And it whistles and talks.

It sits and it stands
And it bends and it kneels,
It sees and it smells,
And it hears and it feels.

It lifts and it carries,
It pulls and it shoves,
It cries and it laughs
And it likes and it loves.

Yes modern machines
May be "fab", "brill" or "hot",
But the HUMAN machine
Is the best of the lot!

Clive Webster

Mum's Time Machine

My Mum invented a *Time Machine*!

It timed how much I moaned and groaned;
It timed how slowly I would dress,
How long it took to brush my teeth –
And how quick my room became a mess.

It timed how long I watched TV,
How little time I sat to eat;
How long I spent on computer games –
And the time I took to wash my feet.

But Mum hadn't planned for one BIG hitch:
The time I took
                    to find the switch!

Trevor Harvey

Giant Crane

It is night
and the city is still.

High above
the building site
and office blocks
the crane
quietly rests
like a huge
diplodocus
ready at dawn
to close its jaws
on breakfast
and lift
a first mouthful
high in the air.

Patricia Leighton

Weather Machine

I've made a machine to control the weather,
so I can have snowflakes, as light as a feather,
whenever I want them. At the flick of a switch.
Snowballs in summer! It should make me rich.

A heatwave in winter. I could choose anything.
Spring showers in autumn, leaves falling in
   spring.
Any weather I please, just press down a key.
The weather I want, when I want it to be.

If there's trouble in class, I shall press "i" for ice,
then they'll close the school. Now that would be
   nice.
When I'm fed up with rain I shall bring out the
   sun.
My machine will be famous. You all will want
   one.

There's only one problem . . .
As hard as I try,
I can't seem to get it
plugged into the sky.

Jane Clarke

Wizard Wobble's Toaster

Wizard Wobble's toaster
Works magic on the bread.
It doesn't turn it into toast
But other things instead.

He puts in two thick slices
Of crusty soft-grain white.
A minute later two fat rabbits
Jump out in a fright.

From Wizard Wobble's toaster
Pop lots of funny things:
A pair of fluffy slippers;
Some goggle-eyes on springs.

A slice of wholemeal granary
Pops out as a bat.
It flits and flies and terrifies
Wizard Wobble's cat.

When Wizard Wobble's hungry
He vacuums up some dust.
His magic vacuum cleaner cooks
A lovely toasty crust.

Celia Warren

Uncle's Robot

My uncle made a robot
And gave it to his nieces.
It walked into a wall,
went CLUNK! and fell to pieces.

Charles Thomson

Formula One Dream Bed

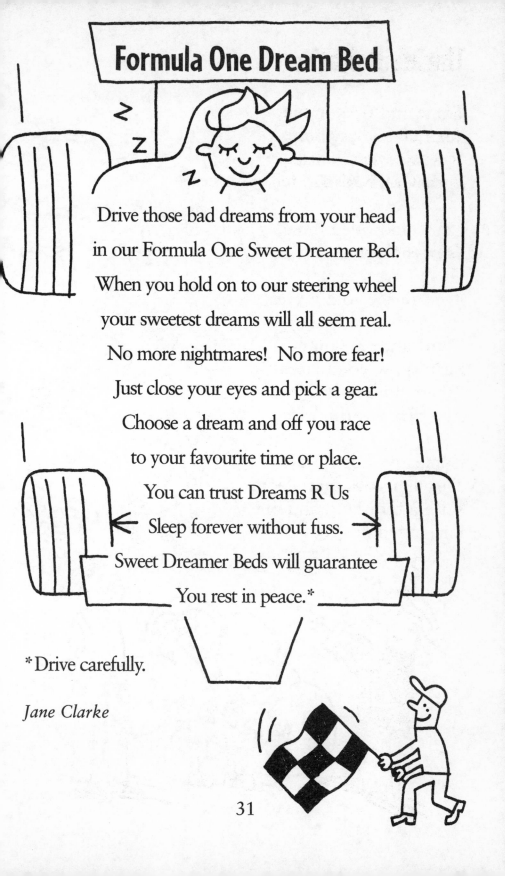

Drive those bad dreams from your head

in our Formula One Sweet Dreamer Bed.

When you hold on to our steering wheel

your sweetest dreams will all seem real.

No more nightmares! No more fear!

Just close your eyes and pick a gear.

Choose a dream and off you race

to your favourite time or place.

You can trust Dreams R Us

Sleep forever without fuss.

Sweet Dreamer Beds will guarantee

You rest in peace.*

*Drive carefully.

Jane Clarke

The Magic Carpet

Come and ride on me,
I can take you where
Wizards weave spells
In the evening air.

Come and ride on me,
I can show you caves
Of shining treasure
Beneath the cold waves.

Come and ride on me,
I can show you places
Where dinosaurs dance
And dragons run races.

Come and ride on me
Through skies that gleam
With a thousand and one
Enchanted dreams.

Cynthia Rider

The Carousel Horse

Round and round,
round and round,
the carousel horse
goes up and down.

With a gilded mane
and a coat of snow,
wild eyes that sparkle
and hooves all aglow,
he gallops to music
that jingles and jars,
and lights flashing
brilliant colours in arcs.

Yet however far
he may seem to go,
he is pinned by steel
to the deck below;
and his great heart aches
(though it does not show)
for rivers and fields
he will never know.

But the girl on his back
who laughs with glee
flies through the air
and is free – is free.

Patricia Leighton

The Road Sweeper Machine

Sweeper, sweeper, clean-road-keeper,
swept my sister – wouldn't keep her!
Spat her from the suction hose
wearing only underclothes!

Gina Douthwaite

The Digger's Song

I'm a digger, a mechanical digger.
With my metal claws
I can scratch, I can scrape
Till I make the earth break.

I'm a digger, a mechanical digger.
With my metal jaws
I can bite, I can tear
Ripping holes anywhere.

I'm a digger, a mechanical digger.
With my metal hands
I can scoop, I can lift.
Whole hills I can shift.

I'm a digger, a mechanical digger.
With my metal teeth
I can snatch, I can seize
Chunks of earth, roots of trees.

I'm a digger, a mechanical digger.
When there's work to be done,
Send for me! I'm the one
Who shifts earth by the ton!

John Foster

Ballooning

When safely in your basket
On a fine ballooning day
It's time to fire the burners up
And cast yourself away.

Climb high above the patchwork fields
And float towards the sky
Then drift a while amongst the clouds
And watch the world pass by.

Richard Caley

Hairdrier

My Mum's hairdrier
buzzes like a bee
Looks like a ray gun
when she points it at me.

"Into the bath now,
Let's shampoo your hair,
then out for a rub down
and a blow of hot air."

It prickles my head
and tingles my ears
It tickles my neck
as it zooms and it whirrs

It whizzes and whooshes
and buzzes at me
It sounds much more like
a bad-tempered bee!

Maggie Holmes

The Famous Iron Queen

Like a roaring dragon
Hissing and steaming,
She rumbles along
Polished and gleaming.

Like a mighty dinosaur
Thunderous and vast,
She makes the earth shake
As she trundles past.

Like a stately goddess
Dressed in gold and green
Comes the fabulous, fire-eating
Famous Iron Queen.

Cynthia Rider

Mrs Sprockett's Strange Machine

Mrs Sprockett has a strange machine.
It will thrill you through and through.
It's got wheels and springs and seven strings
And this is what they do.

Pull string number one . . .
 . . . it begins to hum.
Pull string number two . . .
 . . . it goes **COCK A DOODLE DOO**.
Pull string number three . . .
 . . . it will buzz like a bee zzzzz
Pull string number . . . four . . .
it will start to ROAR.
Pull string number five . . .
 . . . it will dip and **dive**.
Pull string number six
it will play silly tricks.
Pull string number seven . . .
 . . . it will fly up to **heaven**.

Mrs Sprocket has a strange machine.
It will thrill you through and through.
It's got wheels and springs and seven strings
And . . . I WISH I HAD ONE TOO!

Michaela Morgan and Sue Palmer

Night Train

The train
is a shiny caterpillar
in clackety boots
nosing through the blind night,
munching mile after mile
of darkness.

Irene Rawnsley

Professor Plumcake's Wonderful Remote Control

Professor Plumcake's life-long goal
Was to invent the perfect
Remote control!

Press **1** if you want to turn on the lighting,
Press **2** to stop the kids from fighting,
Press **3** to tidy the bedroom floor,
Press **4** to open and shut the door,
Press **5** to rescue the cat from a tree,
Press **6** to make you a cup of tea,
Press **7** to cook you a tasty snack.
Press **8** to scratch your itchy back,
Press **9** to tuck you up safely in bed . . .

"I'm really fed up!"
The professor said.

I expect you're wondering
How that can be . . .

He's lost the remote control
Down the back of the settee!

David Orme

A Mean Machine

It prowls like a predator
Searching out its prey.
It will show no mercy
When things get in its way.

It is always hungry.
This hunter hunts indoors.
It creeps across the carpet
It sweeps over the floors.

It purrs like a panther
It can rattle like a snake.
It wolfs down tiny morsels.
It likes to suck up cake.

Nothing can escape it.
Nothing could be meaner.
Pick up your tiny treasures.
Beware the vacuum cleaner.

Jane Clarke

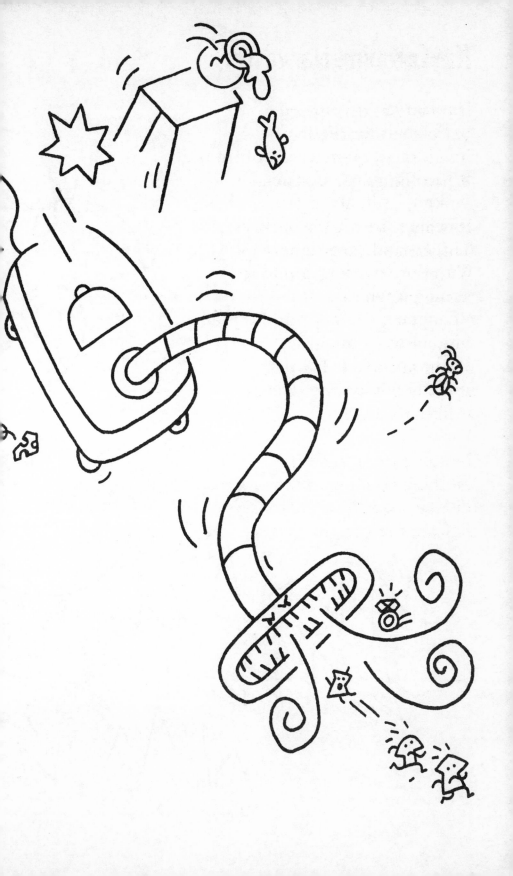

The Combine Harvester

The Harvester rumbled
all through the night.
Small, timid animals ran off in fright
as the big, noisy monster,
winking its lights
crawled through the darkness,
first left and then right.
With dust swirling round it,
turning it white,
it chopped, champed and rattled
with all of its might
till the cornfields lay flat
in the grey morning light.

Marian Swinger

Underground

Is it a worm
rumbling below?
Is it a monster
with nowhere to go?

Is it a mole
lost in the ground?
Just what is
that underground sound?

Is it a creature
from a lost land?
I really can't tell,
I don't understand!

Is it a dragon
digging all day?
Whatever it is
it won't go away.

Is it the gurgling
of a forgotten drain?
Of course, it's just
an underground train!

Andrew Collett

My Rocket Ship

T
Od
Ay I
Made
A rocket ship
That can fly
Me to the stars.
It's made from
Plastic bottles
Cardboard boxes
And jam jars.
Its engine is a
Broken
Clock,
That was left under the stairs.
The seats are made from socks and shirts
That no one   ever wears.

Ian Bland